THE MAYONNAISE COOKBOOK

THE MAYONNAISE COOKBOOK

50 SAVORY AND SWEET RECIPES STARRING THE WORLD'S BEST CONDIMENT

ERIN ISAAC

ULYSSES PRESS

Published in the US by:
ULYSSES PRESS
PO Box 3440
Berkeley, CA 94703
www.ulyssespress.com

ISBN: 978-1-64604-195-4
Library of Congress Control Number: 2021931516

Printed in China
10 9 8 7 6 5 4 3 2 1

Acquisitions editor: Claire Sielaff
Managing editor: Claire Chun
Project editor: Tyanni Niles
Editor: Kathy Kaiser
Proofreader: Renee Rutledge
Production: what!design @ whatweb.com
Cover design and artwork: Rebecca Lown
Interior photographs: shutterstock.com

CONTENTS

CHAPTER THREE

CHAPTER FOUR

CHAPTER FIVE

CHAPTER SIX

I CAN'T BELIEVE IT HAS MAYO! 107

CHAPTER SEVEN

MAYO HACKS 127

CONVERSIONS 130

RECIPE INDEX 132

ABOUT THE AUTHOR 135

iNTRODUCTiON TO MAYONNAiSE

WHAT IS MAYONNAISE? HOW IS IT MADE?

Mayonnaise, also called mayo, is the creamy white condiment that so many people like me just cannot get enough of. It is the most popular condiment in the United States, with sales greater than $2 billion annually, outselling even ketchup and barbecue sauce! Mayo is the most versatile condiment of them all and can be used for so much more than sandwiches. You will find mayo in foods from crab cakes all the way to cupcakes.

So why do we call mayo, mayo? Well, I could bore you with the complex history of mayonnaise, but even after my research I cannot say that I have a straight answer. There are so many different origins. My research took me down a huge rabbit hole, and I ended up somewhere on YouTube watching someone using mayonnaise as a musical instrument. So when you have time to look up the origin of mayonnaise for yourself, choose the scenario that you like best and store it with your other fun facts.

According to *Larousse Gastronomique*, also known as "The World's Greatest Culinary Encyclopedia," mayonnaise can simply be described as this: "A cold sauce of which the basic ingredients are egg yolks in oil blended into an emulsion." In other words, mayonnaise is created by the chemical process of emulsification. I will go into more detail on what emulsification looks like and how to make it later in the cookbook.

WHAT ARE THE DIFFERENT TYPES/BRANDS OF MAYO?

When you go to the condiment aisle in the grocery store, you will see many brands of the same product. Mayo is no different. In my local grocery store, there are more than 25 different types of mayo (yes, I counted), all of which have been commercially prepared to withstand the duration of waiting to be picked up, checked out, and taken to their new home, someone's kitchen. These commercially prepared mayonnaises are composed of the same ingredients as homemade mayo, except they include preservatives, which increase shelf life.

Although all the brands are considered mayonnaise, each is unique. Here is a list and description of the mayonnaise brands I prefer and used while creating this cookbook.

DUKE'S

In my opinion, Duke's mayonnaise has the most neutral and balanced flavor. Duke's can be easily combined with practically any flavor you want, which is why I used it for most of the recipes in this cookbook. Think of Duke's as an empty canvas. Adding a little of this ingredient and a little of that can create a masterpiece. It is also an exceptional substitute ingredient to use in cakes or cupcakes when you do not have any eggs or oil. Duke's is the most versatile of the brands, so you might want to keep it on hand.

HELLMANN'S/BEST FOODS

The texture of Hellmann's (known as Best Foods west of the Rockies) is distinctly different from other types of mayo. It has a light, fluffy, and jiggly texture, almost like Jell-O. Hellmann's has more of a savory taste, which is likely from the amount of mustard it contains. It also seems to be the saltiest of the mayonnaises, which makes it perfect to use to make sauces.

KEWPIE

Out of the three brands of mayonnaise, Kewpie is the tangiest and tastes the strongest. According to Kewpie, there are four egg yolks in every pound of its product, which gives Kewpie a super-rich flavor. This mayonnaise would be best used for making special sauces like the one found on your favorite fast-food burger or in many Asian recipes. (See the Spicy Tuna Poke Bowl, page 87.)

MIRACLE WHIP

Miracle Whip, created in the 1930s, was developed as a contrast to mayonnaise and so is not *technically* a mayonnaise. Miracle Whip is considered to be a whipped dressing as it is much sweeter than mayo. According to the FDA, a certain level of fat content must be present to be considered mayonnaise. Miracle Whip does not meet this criterion; therefore, it is not a mayonnaise. Instead of the fat that mayonnaise has, Miracle Whip contains sugar, ground mustard, and spices, giving it a taste of sweetness with a little spice. It's great for adding sweetness and balance to dishes with strong aromas or flavors, such as tuna salad or egg salad.

DIFFERENCES BETWEEN TYPES OF MAYONNAISE

Although mayo, Miracle Whip, and aioli can be used interchangeably in most dishes, they have different ingredients, which could change the outcome of your dish.

Mayonnaise—This has a thicker consistency and is made of egg yolks, a neutral oil, such as canola oil, and an acidic component, such as lemon juice, vinegar, or sometimes both. You can make your own easily or use Hellmann's, a reliable store-bought option.

Miracle Whip—This whipped dressing contains sugar, ground mustard, and spices. The distinct difference here is a higher sugar content.

Aioli—A strongly flavored, garlicky version of mayonnaise, aioli uses more potently flavorful oils, such as extra-virgin olive oil, with roots tracing back to the mid-nineteenth century.

COMPARING TYPES OF MAYONNAISE

	Egg Yolks	Oil	Garlic	Sweet	Fat Content
Mayonnaise	Yes	Neutral Oil—Canola	No	No	High
Miracle Whip	No	Soybean Oil	Dried Garlic	Yes, contains sugar	Medium
Aioli	Yes	Olive Oil	Fresh Garlic	Sweet ingredients can be added	Low

CHAPTER ONE

HOW TO
MAKE MAYO

Homemade Mayo with Egg

Mayonnaise is made of three ingredients: egg yolk, oil, and some type of acidic component, such as vinegar or lemon. When making homemade mayonnaise, it is important to use a room temperature egg and whisk the egg yolk with the acidic component *before* adding in the olive oil. The acid will help break down the protein in the egg yolk, which will create a better emulsification. The emulsion process forces the oil and acid to mix together.

MAKES: ¼ cup | **PREP TIME:** 5 minutes

1 large pasture-raised egg
at room temperature

juice from ½ lemon

1 cup canola oil

½ teaspoon ground mustard

½ teaspoon salt

¼ teaspoon white pepper

1. Separate the egg yolk from the egg white. Set the egg white aside and add the yolk and lemon juice to a food processor. Pulse continuously until the yolk and lemon juice are well combined.

2. While pulsing, add the oil in a continuous stream. Keep pulsing until the mixture begins to thicken. Then add the ground mustard, salt, and white pepper, and blend until well combined. Taste and add additional salt and pepper as needed.

Pro Tip: Save your egg white for future use. Place the whites into an airtight container and refrigerate for up to one week. Use the whites for egg salad, tuna fish, or even scrambled egg whites.

Homemade Mayo without Egg

Unlike traditional mayo recipes, this homemade vegan mayonnaise does not use an egg or an egg yolk, but instead uses aquafaba, the liquid from a can of chickpeas.

MAKES: ¼ cup | **PREP TIME:** 5 minutes

¼ cup liquid from 1 (15.5-ounce) can chickpeas

½ teaspoon ground mustard

½ teaspoon salt

¼ teaspoon white pepper

juice of ½ lemon

1 cup canola or avocado oil

1. Add all the ingredients to a food processor or blender. Pulse together until well combined. Add more salt to taste and more oil for a thinner consistency.

Garlic-Herb Mayo

This is one of my favorite mayonnaise recipes! The aromatics of the herbs and the acidity of the lemon give this mayo a flavorful and bright taste. Use this to add bold flavor to sandwiches, meat, or even stew! This mayo is also a surprise ingredient in Chicken Pot Pie (page 115).

MAKES: 1½ cups | **PREP TIME:** 5 minutes

½ bunch parsley

1 tablespoon dried oregano

1 tablespoon dried thyme

1 tablespoon dried chives

1½ tablespoons minced garlic

1 tablespoon extra-virgin olive oil

¾ teaspoon salt

½ teaspoon pepper

zest of 1 lemon

juice of 1 lemon

1 cup mayonnaise

1. To a food processor or blender, add all the ingredients except the mayonnaise. Pulse or blend until the mixture is smooth, then transfer to a small mixing bowl.

2. Add the mayonnaise and mix until combined. Refrigerate until ready to serve.

Spicy Mayo

If you want to add a little heat to your mayonnaise, then this recipe is for you. If you like your food extra-spicy, it is okay to use a heavy hand with your hot sauce. Go crazy! This recipe is merely a guide as to how much heat you should add. And if you can't take the heat—then you know the rest!

MAKES: ¾ cup | **PREP TIME:** 5 minutes

½ cup mayonnaise

1 tablespoon hot sauce or sriracha

¼ teaspoon smoked paprika

¼ teaspoon ground chipotle pepper

1. Add all the ingredients to a small bowl and mix until well combined. Serve immediately or chill until ready to serve.

Garlic-Truffle Aioli

Yes, this is the sauce that finds its way onto potatoes, french fries, and burgers in many restaurants these days. And rightfully so, because it enhances each dish and tastes almost surreal! What makes it special is the rich umami flavor from the truffle oil. Fair warning: this aioli is irresistible and will be gone soon after you make it.

MAKES: ½ cup | **PREP TIME:** 5 minutes

¼ cup mayonnaise

¼ cup crème fraîche or sour cream

2 tablespoons white truffle oil

1 teaspoon minced garlic

¼ teaspoon salt

¼ teaspoon white pepper

zest of 1 lemon

squeeze of lemon juice

1. Add all the ingredients to a small bowl. Mix well. Refrigerate until ready to serve.

Ketchup Mayo

The name says it all. This is simply mayonnaise and ketchup mixed with garlic powder and Worcestershire sauce for a little more flavor. This sauce is great as a french fry or tater tot dip. It is also great on a hot dog alongside your favorite toppings.

MAKES: ½ cup | **PREP TIME:** 5 minutes

¼ cup mayonnaise

¼ cup ketchup

dash of garlic powder

dash of Worcestershire sauce

1. Mix all the ingredients in a small bowl. Add more garlic powder to taste. Refrigerate until ready to serve.

Wasabi Mayo

This is my go-to mayo recipe for any type of fish, baked or fried. Yes, there's always tartar sauce, but I like to use this as well because of the spicy kick from the wasabi. This sauce is especially great with fish sticks or as a dip for sushi. Wasabi also has many health benefits, as it contains minerals, including calcium, iron, magnesium, and zinc.

MAKES: ¾ cup | **PREP TIME:** 5 minutes

½ cup mayonnaise

1 teaspoon wasabi paste

1 tablespoon light soy sauce

1 tablespoon agave nectar

juice of ½ lemon

zest of 1 lemon

1. Mix all the ingredients in a small bowl until well combined. Refrigerate until ready to serve.

CHAPTER TWO

APPETIZERS AND DIPS

Angel Eggs

Angel eggs are my version of the popular appetizer deviled eggs. In July 2019 I made these eggs during a live cooking competition at the Ohio State Fair and won second place! Although they did not receive the coveted blue ribbon, my Angel Eggs will always be first place in my eyes—and yours too as soon as you take a bite!

MAKES: 24 angel eggs | **PREP TIME:** 20 minutes | **COOK TIME:** 25 minutes

6 slices thick-cut bacon

1 cup brown sugar

1 dozen large eggs

⅓ cup Miracle Whip

1 tablespoon yellow mustard

3 tablespoons sweet relish

salt

pepper

chopped chives, to serve

CANDIED BACON

1. Preheat the oven to 425°F.

2. Place the bacon flat on a baking sheet lined with parchment paper. Generously cover the slices of bacon with brown sugar.

3. Bake for 15 minutes or until the bacon is fully cooked through and begins to glisten.

4. Remove the bacon from the oven, and set it aside to cool. Finely chop the cooled bacon and set it aside.

EGGS

1. Place the eggs into a large pot of boiling water. Cook for 8 to 10 minutes, until the center is yellow. Note: Do not overcook, which will make the yolks gray. To check if the eggs are cooked, remove an egg from the water, place it on a counter, and give it a spin. If the egg spins, then it's done. If the egg doesn't spin, then return it to the water and finish cooking.

2. Once cooked, run cold water over the eggs. When cool to the touch, peel the eggs and halve them lengthwise. Spoon out the yolks into a medium bowl, and place the egg whites on a serving plate.

3. Add Miracle Whip, mustard, relish, salt, and pepper to the yolks and mix together. Continue adding Miracle Whip and relish until the mixture is a smooth, firm texture and tastes a little sweet. (Be careful not to make it runny.)

4. Once the yolk mixture is smooth, neatly transfer the yolk filling into the white part of the egg. (Note: Place the yolk mixture into a sandwich bag. Cut off the bottom tip of the bag, then squeeze the mixture out through the hole you just created into the white part of the egg.)

5. Keep the eggs chilled until ready to serve. Before serving, top with candied bacon and chives.

Philly Cheesesteak Egg Rolls

Just as the name says, this recipe is a Philly cheesesteak wrapped up inside an egg roll instead of a bun. Flavorful marinated steak with onions, mushrooms, peppers, and cheese are tightly wrapped in an egg roll wrapper and fried until crispy. As soon as you cut into the egg roll, you will see the melted ooey gooey cheese begging to be eaten. I like to dip these in Spicy Mayo (page 21) or Ranch Dressing (page 93), but use your favorite dipping sauce for sure!

MAKES: 10 to 12 egg rolls | **PREP TIME:** 10 minutes, plus
1 hour to marinate | **COOK TIME:** 22 minutes

⅓ cup soy sauce

¼ cup Worcestershire sauce

1 tablespoon Dijon mustard

1 teaspoon minced garlic

1 pound ribeye, sirloin, or top round steak

salt

freshly cracked pepper

1 tablespoon plus 2 cups frying oil
(vegetable or canola oil
works best here)

1 white onion, sliced

1 green pepper, sliced

5 cremini mushrooms, sliced

1 teaspoon flour or cornstarch

1 pack egg roll wrappers

¼ cup mayonnaise

2 to 3 cups Monterey Jack cheese

chopped chives, to serve

1. In a small mixing bowl, combine the soy sauce, Worcestershire sauce, Dijon mustard, and garlic; stir this marinade until well blended and set aside.

2. Place the steak into a ziplock freezer bag, remove the air, then seal. Pound the steak with a meat tenderizer (or a can) until flat. Remove the steak and season both sides liberally with salt and pepper. Place back into the bag and pour in the marinade. Let sit in the refrigerator for at least 1 hour.

3. Add about 1 tablespoon of oil to a medium heated pan. When hot, sear the steak for about 3 minutes on each side. Remove and let rest. Once the steak is cool to the touch, slice it thinly and set aside.

4. In the same pan, toss in the white onion, green pepper, mushrooms, salt, and freshly cracked pepper. Cook on medium heat, stirring occasionally until tender, about 10 minutes. Remove the vegetables from the heat and add the steak. Mix together and set aside.

EGG ROLLS

1. Make the wrapper-sealing mixture by mixing 1 tablespoon of water and 1 teaspoon of flour or cornstarch in a small bowl.

2. Place an egg roll wrapper on a flat surface with a corner pointed toward your body. Spread a small amount of mayo on the wrapper, place a small scoop of steak mixture in the middle, and top with cheese. Add a small amount of sealing mixture to all four sides of the egg roll wrapper. Begin to roll the wrapper away from your body, tuck in the two side corners, and roll the remainder of the way. Place the seal side down, and repeat for the remaining egg rolls.

3. Pour about 2 cups of oil into a medium pan, and heat on medium high. Once the oil is hot, add the egg rolls, seal side down. Cook for 3 minutes on each side or until golden brown.

4. Top with chives and serve hot with your favorite dipping sauce. Mine is the Spicy Mayo (page 21).

French Fries with Garlic-Truffle Aioli

Grab your favorite frozen fries and fry or bake them until slightly brown and crisp, then top the potatoes with Parmesan cheese, parsley, and Garlic-Truffle Aioli. The best part is you will make these fries yourself, and they will be better than most of the fries you have tried at restaurants.

MAKES: 4 servings | **PREP TIME:** 5 minutes | **COOK TIME:** 20 minutes

1 (16-ounce) package frozen seasoned french fries

¼ cup Parmesan cheese, shaved or shredded

½ tablespoon chopped fresh parsley

½ cup Garlic-Truffle Aioli (page 23)

1. Preheat the oven to 425°F. Cook the french fries for 20 minutes or according to the instructions on the package.

2. Once the fries are cooked, toss in as much Parmesan cheese and parsley as you would like. Place them on the serving plates, then generously drizzle the Garlic-Truffle Aioli on top or serve it on the side.

Elote Street Corn

Elote (pronounced *eh-lo-tay*) is Mexican street corn found at fairs, food trucks, and Hispanic restaurants. This recipe will give you savory, spicy, and sweet notes all in one bite. The corn tastes best grilled; however, you can also make it in the oven. And I may be crossing some lines here, but I like to finish mine with Flamin' Hot Cheetos for an extra kick of spice and crunch for texture.

MAKES: 4 full ears of corn or 8 half ears of corn | **PREP TIME:** 5 minutes | **COOK TIME:** 30 minutes

4 ears of corn or 8 frozen half ears

1 to 2 tablespoons extra-virgin olive oil

salt

pepper

¼ cup mayonnaise

¼ cup sour cream

juice of ½ lime

¼ teaspoon cumin

¼ teaspoon chipotle pepper

2 cups cotija cheese

1 cup Flamin' Hot Cheetos (crushed), optional

a few dashes chili-lime seasoning

½ cup chopped cilantro

1. Preheat the oven to 425°F.

2. Rub each ear of corn with olive oil, sprinkle with salt and pepper, and place directly onto a parchment paper–lined baking sheet. Bake the corn for 30 minutes or until it begins to slightly brown. Note: If using a grill, cook on direct heat, flipping continuously until the corn begins to char.

3. In a small bowl, mix the mayonnaise, sour cream, lime juice, cumin, and chipotle pepper. Brush or spoon the mixture onto each ear of corn. Then sprinkle each side liberally with cotija cheese, crushed Flamin' Hot Cheetos, and chili-lime seasoning. Top with cilantro and serve immediately.

Note: To crush the Cheetos, pulse in a food processor until broken into pieces or place in a bag and smash with a can until crushed.

Artichoke and Spinach Dip

Artichoke and spinach dip is a top-five appetizer of all time. The vegetables mixed with the creaminess of the melted cheese make it hard not to like. One of my earliest memories of trying spinach and artichoke dip was as a child. On the weekends, my mom would buy the frozen dips along with tortilla chips, and it would be our delicious snack. I have been trying to perfect this recipe for years, and I think I may have done just that!

MAKES: 8 to 10 servings | **PREP TIME:** 5 minutes | **COOK TIME:** 25 to 30 minutes

1 tablespoon unsalted butter

2 (12-ounce) jars artichoke hearts

2 teaspoons chopped garlic

8 ounces fresh spinach, chopped

1 teaspoon salt

½ teaspoon pepper

½ teaspoon crushed red pepper

½ cup half-and-half

1 (8-ounce) package cream cheese, softened

¼ cup mayonnaise

1 cup white cheddar cheese

¼ cup Parmesan cheese

1 (8-ounce) can water chestnuts

2 tablespoons herb Gournay cheese (optional)

tortilla chips, toast, or veggies, to serve

1. Preheat the oven to 450°F.

2. In a large pan, melt the butter over medium-high heat. Once the butter is melted, add in the artichoke hearts. Cook for 3 minutes, stirring occasionally.

3. Add in the garlic and spinach; cook for an additional 3 minutes, until the spinach begins to wilt. To the same pan, add the salt, pepper, crushed red pepper, and half-and-half. Mix well to combine all the ingredients.

4. Reduce the heat to low, and add in the cream cheese, mayonnaise, white cheddar cheese, Parmesan cheese, and water chestnuts. If you have herb Gournay cheese, add it in now for a pop of flavor.

5. Allow the cheese to melt, and stir occasionally. Once the cheese has melted, taste the dip, and add additional salt to taste or crushed red pepper for more heat. Top with any additional cheese you may have and place in the oven. (Make sure the food is in an oven-safe dish; transfer if necessary.)

6. Cook for 10 to 15 minutes or until the cheese is golden brown and bubbly. Serve hot alongside tortilla chips, toasted pumpernickel bread, or veggies.

Cajun Crab and Shrimp Dip

Not only do I love a good dip, but I also love seafood. When the two are combined, I go straight to food heaven! Whip up this crab and shrimp dip and meet me there!

MAKES: 6 to 8 servings | **PREP TIME:** 5 minutes | **COOK TIME:** 25 minutes

1 tablespoon butter

½ pound medium shrimp, tails off, peeled, and deveined

½ teaspoon Old Bay seasoning

¼ teaspoon Cajun seasoning

¼ teaspoon pepper

juice of ½ lemon

zest of ½ lemon

1 (8-ounce) package cream cheese, softened

½ cup mayonnaise

1 cup sour cream

2 cups Monterey Jack cheese, divided

1 tablespoon chopped fresh parsley

a few dashes of hot sauce

½ pound lump crab meat

butter crackers, tortilla chips, or bread, to serve

1. Preheat the oven to 400°F.

2. Melt the butter over medium-high heat in a medium or large oven-safe pan. Once melted, add the shrimp and cook for 1 minute on each side.

3. Reduce the heat to low, and add the Old Bay seasoning, Cajun seasoning, pepper, lemon juice, and lemon zest. Give the ingredients in the pan a stir.

4. Add the cream cheese, mayo, sour cream, 1 cup of the Monterey Jack cheese, parsley, and hot sauce. Stir continuously and cook until the cheese begins to melt.

5. Gently fold in the crab meat and top with the remaining cheese. Place in the oven for 20 minutes or until the cheese begins to brown and bubble.

6. Serve immediately with butter crackers or your favorite tortilla chips.

Buffalo Chicken Dip

Buffalo chicken dip is a popular dip that shows up at many gatherings, and I always gravitate toward it. This is a great way to use leftover chicken or turkey from the holidays.

MAKES: 8 to 10 servings | **PREP TIME:** 5 minutes | **COOK TIME:** 30 minutes

2½ cups cooked chicken or turkey, shredded or chopped (use a rotisserie chicken, leftover chicken, or whatever chicken you like)

½ (8 ounce) package cream cheese, softened

2 cups shredded Monterey Jack cheese, divided

¼ cup mayonnaise

1 cup hot sauce

½ cup blue cheese dressing

1 (4-ounce) can green chiles, diced

1 teaspoon minced garlic

¼ teaspoon smoked paprika

¼ teaspoon salt

¼ teaspoon pepper

squeeze of lemon juice

tortilla chips, toast, or veggies, to serve

1. Preheat the oven to 400°F.

2. To a 1- to 2-quart oven-safe dish, add all the ingredients except 1 cup of the Monterey Jack cheese. Mix until well combined. Place the dip in the oven and cook for 20 minutes.

3. Remove the dip from the oven, stir, and scrape the sides. Top with the remaining Monterey Jack cheese.

4. Return to the oven and cook for an additional 10 minutes or until the cheese begins to brown and bubble.

5. Serve hot with tortilla chips, toast, or veggies.

Caramelized French Onion Dip

This recipe is what happens when you put French onion dip and French onion soup together. You get the creaminess from French onion dip and the beefy, oniony flavor and texture of French onion soup for the perfect sharable appetizer.

MAKES: 4 to 6 servings | **PREP TIME:** 5 minutes | **COOK TIME:** 25 to 28 minutes

2 tablespoons butter

1 tablespoon extra-virgin olive oil, preferably garlic infused

2 sweet onions, thinly sliced

½ teaspoon salt

½ teaspoon pepper

1 tablespoon sherry vinegar

2 cloves garlic, minced

1 envelope onion soup mix

½ cup beef broth

¼ cup mayonnaise

1 cup sour cream

½ cup white cheddar cheese, shredded

¼ cup Parmesan cheese, grated, shredded, or shaved

potato chips, to serve

1. In a large pan, melt the butter over medium-high heat. Once the butter is melted, add the olive oil, followed by the onions, salt, and pepper. Stir the onion slices in the pan, making sure to coat them all with the butter-oil mixture. Spread the onions out flat on the surface of the pan and cook for about 2 minutes. Stir and reduce the heat to medium, then cook an additional 8 to 10 minutes, stirring occasionally, making sure not to burn the onions.

2. Once the onions have softened and begin to brown, add the sherry vinegar, garlic, and onion soup mix, and stir well. Cook for an additional 1 minute, then reduce the heat to medium.

3. Add the beef broth, mayonnaise, sour cream, white cheddar cheese, and Parmesan cheese. Cook until all the cheese is melted and begins to warm. Taste and add additional salt and cheese to your liking.

4. Serve hot alongside potato chips.

Pimiento Cheese

Pimiento cheese is a spread that is extremely popular in the South. It can be served in sandwiches, with crackers, or even stuffed inside other foods (see Pimiento Cheese–Stuffed Burgers, page 65). It is packed with flavor, and if you are a cheese lover like me, you will adore the taste.

MAKES: 4 cups | **PREP TIME:** 5 minutes

1 (8-ounce) package cream cheese, softened

⅓ cup mayonnaise

2 cups cheddar cheese

4 tablespoons pimientos, drained

1 jalapeño pepper, finely diced

½ teaspoon garlic powder

¼ teaspoon smoked paprika

¼ teaspoon salt

¼ teaspoon pepper

crackers or veggies, to serve

1. Add all the ingredients to a food processor and pulse until well blended. Serve alongside your favorite crackers or veggies.

CHAPTER THREE

SANDWICHES

Fish Fillet Sandwich

This is a classic fish fillet sandwich on a bun with cheddar cheese and tartar sauce. Add wasabi mayo for a little razzle-dazzle.

MAKES: 4 sandwiches | **PREP TIME:** 10 minutes | **COOK TIME:** 6 to 8 minutes

4 fillets white fish (I used haddock, but cod would also work here)

½ cup all-purpose flour

1 egg, separated

1 cup Italian breadcrumbs

½ teaspoon onion powder

½ teaspoon garlic powder

½ teaspoon paprika

1 teaspoon salt

½ teaspoon pepper

juice from ½ lemon

½ cup buttermilk

2 cups canola oil

4 slices cheddar cheese

2 tablespoons butter (optional)

4 buns

Tartar Sauce (page 101), to serve

Wasabi Mayo (page 27), to serve (optional)

1. Rinse the fish fillets, under cool water, thoroughly pat dry with a paper towel or napkin, and then set aside.

2. Add the flour, egg white, and breadcrumbs to three separate bowls, each one large enough to fit the fish. To the bowl with the flour, add the onion powder, garlic powder, paprika, salt, and pepper, and stir together. To the egg bowl, add the lemon juice and egg yolk. Whisk until well combined, then pour in the buttermilk.

3. Heat the oil in a medium frying pan over medium heat. As the pan is heating, coat the fish with the flour mixture. Next, dip the fish into the egg mixture. Finally, dip the fish into the breadcrumbs. Once the oil is hot, add the fish and cook for 3 to 4 minutes on each side until browned.

4. Remove the fish from the oil and place it on a paper towel to drain off the excess oil. Top with cheese.

5. Spread butter, if using, on the buns, and toast them under a broiler on high heat until browned. Remove the buns and add the fish. Top with Tartar Sauce, Wasabi Mayo, if using, and any other toppings you would like. Serve hot!

Spicy Chicken Sandwich

Remember when Popeyes, the popular chicken joint, released their chicken sandwich, and the lines wrapped around the corner and down the street? Well, I certainly do because I was one of those people waiting to try that delicious goodness. This recipe is my take on that chicken sandwich, but with pepper jack cheese, tomato, and lettuce added. I hope I did the original justice!

MAKES: 2 sandwiches | **PREP TIME:** 10 minutes, plus 1 hour to overnight to marinate | **COOK TIME:** 10 to 15 minutes

1 cup buttermilk

¼ cup hot sauce

2 chicken breasts

1½ cups flour

½ teaspoon garlic powder

1 teaspoon paprika

1½ teaspoons salt

1 teaspoon pepper

2½ cups canola oil

pepper jack cheese, sliced

1 tablespoon butter

2 buns

½ cup Spicy Mayo (page 21)

2 tomatoes, sliced

4 to 6 pickles

2 pieces lettuce

1. Mix the buttermilk and hot sauce in a medium bowl, then add the chicken breasts and cover. Refrigerate and marinate for at least 1 hour; you will get the best results if you marinate the chicken overnight. An hour before frying, remove the chicken from the refrigerator to bring it to room temperature.

2. When you are ready to fry, mix the flour, garlic powder, paprika, salt, and pepper in a small bowl.

3. Heat the oil in a medium or large frying pan over medium heat. As the pan is heating, coat the chicken with the flour mixture. Once the oil is hot, add the chicken and cook for 4 to 5 minutes on each side or until the chicken is cooked through. Remove the chicken from the oil and place it on a paper towel to drain off excess oil. (Note: Chicken should be cooked to an internal temperature of at least 155°F but no greater than 165°F, to prevent it from drying out.) Top with the cheese.

4. Butter the buns and toast them under a broiler on high heat until browned. Remove and add the chicken to the bun, along with the Spicy Mayo, tomato, pickles, and lettuce.

Lobster Roll

This recipe makes me feel like I am sitting somewhere on the East Coast enjoying life! A lobster roll is simply cooked lobster meat (typically a mix of claw, knuckle, and tail meat) tossed with mayonnaise, lemon, and other ingredients of the cook's choice. I was amazed at how well all the ingredients worked together to elevate the lobster and help it taste as fresh as if I had caught it myself. This is my favorite sandwich in this cookbook!

MAKES: 2 to 3 lobster rolls, depending on the bun size
| **PREP TIME:** 10 minutes | **COOK TIME:** 10 minutes

5 cups water

1 tablespoon seafood seasoning

½ lemon, sliced

juice of ½ lemon

4 (4-ounce) lobster tails

1 stalk celery, finely diced

½ red bell pepper, finely diced

1 teaspoon chopped tarragon

2 tablespoons chopped chives

1 teaspoon lemon juice

zest of ½ lemon

¼ cup mayonnaise

¼ teaspoon smoked paprika

¼ teaspoon salt

½ teaspoon pepper

2 tablespoons butter

3 brioche buns

1. To a medium pot, add the water, seafood seasoning, lemon slices, and lemon juice, and stir. Bring the water to a boil over medium-high heat.

2. Once the water is boiling, add the lobster tails and cook for 5 minutes. Remove the lobster tails from the pot and rinse under cold water, or place in a medium bowl with ice and water until the lobster tails are cool. Discard the rest of the contents of the pot.

3. Once the lobster tail is cool to the touch, slice open the bottom of the lobster tail and remove the white meat.

4. Roughly chop the lobster meat, and place it into a large mixing bowl. Add the celery, red bell pepper, tarragon, chives, lemon juice, lemon zest, mayo, smoked paprika, salt, and pepper; mix until well combined. Add more salt and pepper to taste. Refrigerate the lobster salad until ready to serve.

5. Butter the brioche buns and toast them under a broiler on high heat until browned. Remove the buns and add the lobster. Top with additional chopped chives or tarragon, if desired.

Turkey Club Sandwich

Unlike a classic club sandwich, this one isn't a double decker—but in my humble opinion, this sandwich is flawless. Switch it up according to your mood by using different types of mayonnaise and cheese. Add more turkey deli meat if you like it stacked high.

MAKES: 2 sandwiches | **PREP TIME:** 5 minutes | **COOK TIME:** 5 minutes

mayonnaise

4 slices whole wheat or multigrain bread

butter

4 to 6 slices smoked turkey deli meat,

2 slices Swiss cheese

4 to 6 slices cooked bacon

1 large tomato, sliced

2 pieces lettuce

1. Spread as much or as little mayonnaise as you would like onto one side of each slice of bread.

2. In a pan large enough to fit the bread, melt the butter over medium heat. When the butter is melted, add the bread slices, mayo side up.

3. Place the turkey in the pan to heat. Once the turkey is warm, move it onto each slice of bread and top with the cheese. Continue cooking until the bread turns golden brown and a slice of cheese is melted.

4. Remove from the pan and top with bacon, tomato, and lettuce. Stack the two slices of bread together to make a sandwich and slice in half. Repeat with the remaining two slices of bread. Serve immediately.

Tuna Melt

Tuna melts were always a hit in our house when I was growing up and possibly one of the first hot sandwiches I learned how to cook. The recipe calls for cheddar cheese, but you can use whatever kind of cheese you like here to make it your own.

MAKES: 2 sandwiches | **PREP TIME:** 5 minutes | **COOK TIME:** 5 minutes

1 tablespoon butter

4 slices bread

1 cup Tuna Salad (page 75)

4 slices cheddar cheese

1. In a pan large enough to fit all four slices of bread, melt the butter over medium heat. Once melted, add the bread and cook until browned. Flip the bread over and toast the opposite side.

2. Place one slice of cheese onto each slice of bread, then spread the tuna on top of two of the slices.

3. Once the cheese begins to melt, place the slices of bread without the tuna onto the slices of bread with the tuna to form a sandwich.

4. Continue cooking until both sides of the sandwiches are completely browned and the cheese is melted. Serve immediately.

Patty Melt

A patty melt is top-tier diner food and one of my favorite ways to eat a burger. The melty cheese, along with the tangy onions and Thousand Island dressing, is a helluva combo!

MAKES: 4 patty melts | **PREP TIME:** 5 minutes | **COOK TIME:** 12 to 14 minutes

1 pound ground turkey or ground beef

1 teaspoon salt

½ teaspoon pepper

2 tablespoons Thousand Island dressing, plus more for serving

1 to 2 tablespoons extra-virgin olive oil

8 slices Swiss cheese

1 onion, sliced

1 (16-ounce) container fresh mushrooms, sliced

1 to 2 tablespoons butter

½ cup mayonnaise, or 1 tablespoon per slice of bread

8 slices bread

1. Add the ground turkey or beef to a large bowl, along with salt, pepper, and 2 tablespoons of Thousand Island dressing. Gently mix until all the ingredients are well combined.

2. Divide the meat into four equal sections and form circular patties with your hand. Then smash them down, flattening them enough to fit the size of your bread.

3. In a large pan, heat 1 tablespoon of extra-virgin olive oil over medium-high heat. Once the pan and olive oil are both hot, add the burger patties and cook for 3 to 4 minutes per side.

4. Remove the patties from the pan, set them aside, and top each one with a slice of cheese. Add a little more olive oil to the same pan, along with the onion and mushrooms. Sprinkle with a little salt and cook for about 5 minutes, stirring occasionally, until the onion and mushrooms are browned.

5. In a clean pan or griddle over medium heat, melt about 1 tablespoon of butter or enough to coat the bottom. Slather the mayo onto both sides of each slice of bread, then place in the pan and cook for about 1 minute or until the bread begins to brown.

6. Flip the bread over and place a slice of cheese on the toasted side of four slices of bread. On top of the cheese, add the onion and mushrooms, followed by the patty. Top with Thousand Island dressing and place another slice of bread on top.

7. Use a spatula to smash down the tops of the sandwiches. Flip to make sure both sides of each sandwich are toasted and browned. Slice each sandwich in half and serve immediately.

BLT—Bacon, Lettuce, and Tomato Sandwich

This is simply a classic bacon, lettuce, and tomato sandwich, better known as the BLT. I like to use Miracle Whip for this sandwich because its sweetness, combined with the saltiness of the bacon, creates a party in your mouth. Mayo works for this sandwich as well. Use Garlic-Herb Mayo (page 19) or Wasabi Mayo (page 27) to spruce it up a bit.

MAKES: 2 sandwiches | **PREP TIME:** 10 minutes

½ cup Miracle Whip

4 slices bread

6 to 8 slices cooked bacon

2 pieces lettuce

1 tomato, sliced

sprinkle of salt and pepper (optional)

1. Spread the Miracle Whip onto one side of each slice of bread. Add as much bacon, lettuce, and tomato as you would like to two slices of bread.

2. Sprinkle a little salt and pepper, if using, on the tomato.

3. Place another slice on top of each of the two loaded slices of bread, making two sandwiches. Cut each sandwich in half and serve.

Pimiento Cheese-Stuffed Burgers

Imagine biting into a burger and tasting a bomb of savory and flavorful cheese! Well, that is exactly what you will get with this recipe. Make the Pimiento Cheese recipe (page 47), then stuff the cheese inside the burgers! Cook the patties right away, or freeze and save for later.

MAKES: 4 burgers | **PREP TIME:** 5 minutes | **COOK TIME:** 8 to 10 minutes

1-pound ground beef chuck (80/20)

½ teaspoon Worcestershire sauce

½ teaspoon Dijon mustard

2 tablespoons Italian breadcrumbs

1 teaspoon salt

½ teaspoon pepper

4 (½-tablespoon) cubes pimiento cheese (place in freezer before cooking), plus more for serving

1 tablespoon extra-virgin olive oil

4 of your favorite burger buns

4 pieces lettuce

4 slices tomato

1. Add the ground beef, Worcestershire sauce, Dijon mustard, breadcrumbs, salt, and pepper to a large bowl. Gently mix until all of the ingredients are well combined.

2. Divide the meat into four equal sections and begin to form circular patties with your hand. Make a small dent in the middle of each patty and place a pimiento cheese cube in it. Continue to form the patty, making sure to tuck and hide the pimiento cheese inside the patty.

3. Add extra-virgin olive oil to a large pan over medium-high heat. Once the pan and olive oil are hot, add the burger patties and cook for 3 to 4 minutes per side. Remove the patties from the pan and place on the burger buns. Top with your favorite burger toppings, finish with the top bun, and serve immediately.

> **Pro Tip:** These burger patties are great for make-ahead meals! Simply form the patties and place them in a freezer-safe bag, separating each patty with parchment paper. Store for up to 3 months. When ready to eat, remove from the freezer and place in the fridge to let thaw. When thawed, cook according to the instructions in the recipe.

CHAPTER FOUR

SALADS

Potato Salad

Potato salad is a dish that many look forward to at cookouts and other summer gatherings. But let's be honest, everyone's potato salad is different, and some are simply better than others. This recipe is one that everyone will love and that has a good base so you can add any of your favorite ingredients without unduly compromising the flavor. Use Miracle Whip in this recipe to add a sweet and tangy flavor.

MAKES: 8 to 10 servings | **PREP TIME:** 15 minutes | **COOK TIME:** 25 minutes

3 pounds Yukon gold potatoes, quartered (peel or keep skin on, your preference)

4 hard-boiled eggs, diced

1½ cups Miracle Whip

2 tablespoons yellow mustard

1 tablespoon pimientos

¼ cup sweet relish

1 sweet onion, finely diced, divided

1 celery stalk, finely diced

1 teaspoon salt

½ teaspoon pepper

paprika (optional)

1. Add the potatoes to a large pot and fill it with enough cold water to cover them. Bring to a boil over medium-high heat. Cook for about 20 minutes or until the potatoes become fork-tender (easily pierced with a fork). Drain the water and set the potatoes aside to cool. Note: Let the potatoes cool fully before combining them with the other ingredients.

2. Once cool, add the potatoes to a large bowl along with the eggs. In a small bowl, combine the Miracle Whip, mustard, pimientos, relish, half of the onion, celery, salt, and pepper. Mix, then add the mixture to the potatoes and eggs.

3. Add more salt, pepper, or onion to taste. For a creamier texture, add in additional mayo and relish.

4. Sprinkle the paprika, if using, liberally on top. Refrigerate until ready to serve.

> **Pro Tip:** Make the potato salad ahead of time to let the flavors marry. It's best if it's made the day before and sits overnight in the refrigerator.

Rotisserie Chicken Salad

Rotisserie chicken is my go-to protein whenever I want to make a quick meal. Buying the chicken precooked cuts way down on prep time. I like to use rotisserie chicken in many dishes, including soups, stir fries, and sandwiches. Or I might simply leave it as is and dip it into something saucy. One of my favorite ways to transform a rotisserie chicken is by making chicken salad. This recipe reminds me of lunches from my childhood. We ate chicken salad often, but somehow I never got tired of it. My mom would take leftover chicken from the prior day's meal and use it to make chicken salad with Miracle Whip. Here is her recipe, but with mayo instead of Miracle Whip and rotisserie chicken instead of home-cooked chicken breast.

MAKES: 3 cups or 4 to 6 servings | **PREP TIME:** 15 minutes

2 cups rotisserie chicken, chopped
(I use a breast, thighs, and legs)

1 cup mayonnaise

1 large Honeycrisp apple, diced

⅔ cup red grapes, diced (about 20 grapes)

1 cup golden raisins

juice of 1 lemon

1 teaspoon salt

½ teaspoon pepper

1. Using a fork, remove the chicken breast, thighs, and legs from the rotisserie chicken. Roughly chop the chicken meat.

2. To a large mixing bowl, add the chopped chicken, mayo, apple, grapes, raisins, lemon juice, salt, and pepper. Stir together until well combined. Taste and add additional mayo, salt, or pepper as needed.

Lobster Salad

Fresh and flavorful lobster salad is a delight. But if lobster is not your thing, use cooked shrimp instead. You will need about 1 pound of shrimp to substitute for the lobster in this recipe.

MAKES: 2 to 3 cups | **PREP TIME:** 15 minutes | **COOK TIME:** 10 minutes

5 cups water

1 tablespoon seafood seasoning

½ lemon, sliced

juice of ½ lemon

4 (4-ounce) lobster tails

1 stalk celery, finely diced

½ red bell pepper, finely diced

1 teaspoon chopped tarragon

2 tablespoons chopped chives

1 teaspoon lemon juice

zest of ½ lemon

¼ cup mayonnaise

¼ teaspoon smoked paprika

¼ teaspoon salt

½ teaspoon pepper

1. Add the water, seafood seasoning, sliced lemon, and lemon juice to a medium pot. Give the contents of the pot a stir and bring to a boil over medium-high heat. Once boiling, add the lobster tails and cook for 5 minutes. Remove the lobster tails from the pot. Discard the rest of the contents of the pot. Rinse under cold water, or place in a large bowl with ice and water until the lobster tail is cooled.

2. Once the lobster tail is cool to the touch, remove the white meat by slicing open the bottom of the lobster tail.

3. Roughly chop the lobster meat and place it in a large mixing bowl. Add the celery, red bell pepper, tarragon, chives, lemon juice, lemon zest, mayo, smoked paprika, salt, and pepper; mix until well combined. Add additional salt and pepper to taste. Refrigerate the lobster salad until ready to serve.

Tuna Salad

This tuna salad is better than anything you'll find at the deli. Trust me, I've turned tuna haters into believers with this one! The Miracle Whip, along with the relish, bring sweetness to the dish, counterbalancing the pungent flavor from the fish.

MAKES: 4 cups | **PREP TIME:** 20 minutes

4 (5-ounce) cans tuna fish in water, drained

2 hard-boiled eggs, chopped

1 cup Miracle Whip

½ cup sweet relish

6 to 8 bread-and-butter pickles, chopped

3 teaspoons bread-and-butter pickle juice

3 green onions, chopped and hairy bottoms removed

squeeze of lemon juice

¼ teaspoon salt

¼ teaspoon pepper

crackers or bread, to serve

1. Using a spoon, scoop the tuna into in a medium bowl. Add in all the other ingredients and mix until well combined. Refrigerate until ready to eat.

2. Serve with crackers or bread, or use in a Tuna Melt (page 59).

Egg Salad

Calling all egg lovers! This egg salad is creamy and flavorful. The Miracle Whip and pickles give it an added sweetness. The best part about it is that it is quite simple and easy to make.

MAKES: 2 to 3 cups | **PREP TIME:** 5 minutes | **COOK TIME:** 20 minutes

5 cups water

6 eggs

2 tablespoons Miracle Whip

1 tablespoon Dijon mustard

1 teaspoon yellow mustard

¼ cup bread-and-butter pickles, chopped

1 tablespoon bread-and-butter pickle juice

½ small yellow onion, finely diced

½ teaspoon salt

¼ teaspoon pepper

1 dash hot sauce

sprinkle of dried dill (optional)

sprinkle of paprika (optional)

crackers or toast, to serve

1. Add the water and eggs to a small pot. Cook over medium-high heat for 20 minutes. (Pro Tip: To check whether an egg is boiled, simply set it on a flat surface and try to spin it. If it spins, then it is boiled.)

2. Rinse the eggs under cold water and peel each one. Once peeled, cut the eggs in half, and separate the yolks from the whites. In a small bowl use a fork or spoon to smash the yolks until almost smooth. Chop the egg whites and add to the smashed yolks.

3. Now add the Miracle Whip, Dijon mustard, yellow mustard, pickles, pickle juice, onion, salt, pepper, and hot sauce. Gently mix until all the ingredients are combined. Top with a sprinkle of dill and paprika, if using, and refrigerate until ready to serve.

4. Serve with crackers or on toast.

Wedge Salad

Iceberg is a simple, bland lettuce. But what it lacks in taste, it makes up for in crunchiness and price (the average price of a head is an affordable $1). One of my favorite ways to use a head of iceberg is by creating a wedge salad. There is just something about it being doused with lemon juice, sprinkled with many toppings, and drizzled with dressing that transforms it into the most delicious bite. The recipe with measurements is below, but honestly, just top the iceberg with how much of each ingredient you want. There is no such thing as too much with this one.

MAKES: 2 to 4 servings (two halves or four quarters) | **PREP TIME:** 10 minutes

1 head iceberg lettuce, rinsed and cut into quarters or halves

juice of ½ lemon

½ teaspoon pepper

6 grape tomatoes, sliced

4 strips cooked bacon, crumbled

1 tablespoon blue cheese

1 green onion, sliced

Ranch Dressing (page 93)

1. Cut the head of iceberg lettuce into quarters or halves. Gently rinse under cold water and pat dry with a paper towel.

2. Place the lettuce sections on a serving dish or plates.

3. Squeeze lemon juice on top of each lettuce section, then sprinkle with pepper. Top with the grape tomatoes, crumbled bacon, blue cheese, and green onion. Drizzle on Ranch Dressing and serve immediately.

HOW TO MAKE THE PERFECT BACON

One of the easiest ways to cook bacon is in the oven. This method of cooking helps bacon get extra crispy and cook evenly. It is also a great way to prepare a large quantity of bacon in a short time. All you need is bacon, aluminum foil, and a baking sheet. Preheat the oven to 425°F. Then line a baking sheet with the foil. Place the bacon strips directly on the foil, keeping a little space in between each strip. Bake for 12 minutes or until the bacon begins to crisp or reach your desired doneness. Transfer the bacon with a fork to a paper towel or baking rack to drain off excess grease.

Seven-Layer Salad

The seven-layer salad is one of the most visually pleasing salads when placed in a clear bowl. Seeing how all the layers look when stacked on top of each other makes it so hard to even want to dig in and take a bite. But when you finally do, the flavors from the different layers will make you so glad you did!

MAKES: about 6 to 8 servings | **PREP TIME:** 20 minutes

8 ounces shredded lettuce

1 (8.5-ounce) can peas, drained, or 1 cup frozen peas, thawed

3 hard-boiled eggs, sliced

dash of salt

dash of pepper

2 cups cheddar cheese, shredded

2 to 3 cups cooked chicken or turkey, cubed or shredded

1 (12-ounce) jar sliced roasted red peppers, drained

1 (8.75-ounce) can whole kernel corn

1 to 2 cups Ranch Dressing (page 93)

4 to 6 basil leaves, roughly chopped

1. Add the lettuce to a large clear bowl. Arrange so that the entire bottom of the bowl is covered to create the first layer. Add the second layer of peas, arranging them so that they lie flat on top of the first layer.

2. Next add the eggs, then sprinkle a thin layer of salt and pepper on top. Follow this layer with cheddar cheese. Then add the chicken or turkey, followed by the red peppers and corn. Top with Ranch Dressing and finish with basil on top.

3. Finally, take a step back and admire your creation (this is my favorite part of making this salad). Refrigerate until ready to serve.

BLT SEVEN-LAYER SALAD

Turn the classic bacon, lettuce, and tomato sandwich into a delicious seven-layer salad! To a clear bowl, add these ingredients in this order: 1 head chopped iceberg lettuce, 2 cups halved grape tomatoes, 2 chopped avocados (squeeze some lime over this layer), 1 bunch chopped green onions, 1 bunch chopped cilantro, Ranch Dressing (page 93), 2 cups shredded cheddar cheese, and ½ to 1 cup cooked, chopped bacon.

Macaroni Salad

This classic macaroni salad is packed with fresh flavor. It is a great addition to any cookout or gathering in the summer. Make it the night before to allow the flavors to marry overnight.

MAKES: 8 to 10 servings | **PREP TIME:** 15 minutes | **COOK TIME:** 10 minutes

4 cups dry elbow macaroni

1 celery stalk, diced

½ red bell pepper, diced

3 green onions, chopped

1 clove garlic, chopped

¼ cup mayonnaise

½ cup sour cream

juice and zest of 1 lemon

1 teaspoon salt

¾ teaspoon pepper

1. Cook the macaroni according to the package instructions. Drain, rinse, and add to a large mixing bowl.

2. To the same bowl, add the celery, red bell pepper, green onions, garlic, mayo, sour cream, lemon juice, lemon zest, salt, and pepper. Gently mix until all the ingredients are well combined.

3. Add additional salt to taste. Refrigerate until ready to serve.

Variation: For a delicious twist, add chunks of smoked salmon (2 to 4 ounces) to the salad in step 2. Be careful to keep the chunks intact when mixing.

Coleslaw

A simple cabbage coleslaw to add to hot dogs, burgers, or tacos for a crunchy texture and a cool finish.

MAKES: 4 servings (3 cups) | **PREP TIME:** 10 minutes

1 cup shredded red cabbage

2 cups shredded Napa cabbage

2 stalks green onion, chopped

1 tablespoon chopped cilantro

1 jalapeño, diced

juice of 1 lime

1 tablespoon Miracle Whip

1 tablespoon honey

½ teaspoon chili-lime seasoning or ¼ teaspoon salt

1. Add all the ingredients to a large bowl and gently mix until well combined. Cover and refrigerate until ready to serve.

My absolute favorite thing to eat coleslaw on is a Polish boy, a beef sausage sandwich native to Cleveland, Ohio. A Polish boy is served on a bun with a grilled or fried Polish or kielbasa sausage link. The link is topped with french fries, barbecue sauce, and coleslaw. It is a delicious mess of a sandwich that I just cannot get enough of. If you are ever in Cleveland, I highly recommend giving it a try!

Spicy Tuna Poke Bowl

Spicy tuna poke bowls are easy to whip up! Serve the poke over salad greens for a light lunch, or with rice for a more filling meal.

MAKES: 2 bowls | **PREP TIME:** 15 minutes | **COOK TIME:** 4 minutes

1 tablespoon extra-virgin olive oil

3 sushi-grade ahi tuna steaks

dash of salt

dash of pepper

1 green onion, chopped

Kewpie mayo or Spicy Mayo (page 21)

squeeze of lime juice

2 cups cooked brown rice or mixed greens

1 carrot, julienned

½ seedless cucumber, julienned

1 avocado, thinly sliced

dash of everything bagel seasoning or furikake

4 to 6 sushi nori sheets

soy sauce, to serve

1. In a medium skillet large enough to fit the tuna, heat the olive oil over medium-high heat. Liberally season both sides of the tuna steaks with salt and pepper.

2. Place the tuna in the pan and sear the first side for 2 minutes, until lightly browned. Flip the tuna and sear for 2 minutes or until the tuna is cooked to your preferred doneness. (I prefer my tuna fillets with a pink center.)

3. Remove from the skillet and let rest. Once the tuna is cool to the touch, dice and add to a medium bowl.

4. To the bowl with the tuna, add the green onion, as much Kewpie or Spicy Mayo as you would like, and a squeeze of lime juice. Stir the ingredients together; set aside.

5. In medium serving bowls, add in brown rice or mixed greens, then top with the tuna mixture, carrot, cucumber, and avocado. Sprinkle everything bagel seasoning or furikake on top. Serve immediately alongside nori sheets and soy sauce.

Note: While this recipe calls for searing the tuna steaks, you can skip the skillet, cube the sushi-grade fish, add it to a medium bowl, then sprinkle with salt and pepper. Continue with step 4 above.

CHAPTER FIVE

DRESSINGS AND SAUCES

Caesar Dressing

There are many restaurants that will whip up a Caesar salad with dressing tableside, such as my personal favorite, La Dolce Vita in Detroit, Michigan. They bring a wooden bowl on a cart next to your dining table and begin by chopping up anchovies. It is quite a memorable experience. Another way to indulge in a great Caesar salad is by creating the dressing yourself. This recipe packs fabulous flavor and will adjust your taste buds to never want a store-bought Caesar dressing again!

MAKES: 1½ cups or 12 ounces | **PREP TIME:** 10 minutes

1 cup mayonnaise

2 teaspoons Dijon mustard

1 teaspoon Worcestershire sauce

1½ teaspoons anchovy paste

1 teaspoon garlic

½ cup grated Parmesan cheese

juice of ½ lemon

zest of ½ lemon

¼ teaspoon salt

¼ teaspoon pepper

1. Add all the ingredients to a medium mixing bowl and mix until well combined. Add in additional Parmesan cheese, salt, or pepper to your taste.

PERFECT PAIRING

Caesar Salad—On top of a bed of romaine lettuce, add your favorite protein, tomatoes, Parmesan cheese, black pepper, croutons, and Caesar dressing.

Chicken Caesar Wrap—Add cooked chicken to a tortilla wrap, along with a white cheese (Parmesan or white cheddar cheese work best here), sliced tomatoes, shredded lettuce, and Caesar dressing. Roll all of the ingredients inside the wrap and serve cold.

Ranch Dressing

Fun Fact: Ranch is the *most* consumed salad dressing in the United States. Many put it on anything, from salad to pizza to potatoes. There are so many ways to make ranch dressing. Here is my version of it, and it is scrumptious!

MAKES: 1½ cups or 12 ounces | **PREP TIME:** 5 minutes

1 cup mayonnaise

¼ cup buttermilk

½ teaspoon dried dill

2 teaspoons dried chives

1 teaspoon dried parsley

¼ teaspoon garlic powder

¼ teaspoon onion powder

¼ teaspoon smoked paprika

¼ teaspoon ground mustard

½ teaspoon salt

¼ teaspoon pepper

squeeze of lemon juice

1. Add all the ingredients to a medium mixing bowl. Whisk vigorously until well combined. Refrigerate until ready to serve.

Pro Tip: To make this dressing dairy free and vegan, use vegan mayonnaise and dairy-free milk, such as almond milk, cashew milk, or oat milk.

SRIRACHA RANCH SAUCE

Spice it up! Sriracha ranch is a sauce I like to make for dipping. Simply add ranch dressing to a small bowl with as much sriracha as you would like. Mix until well combined. The more sriracha you add, the hotter the sauce will be.

Blue Cheese Dressing

One of the benefits of making homemade dressing is knowing exactly what is in it and having total control over it. I love making blue cheese dressing at home because I get to add a copious amount of blue cheese crumbles to make the flavor really pop.

MAKES: 2 cups | **PREP TIME:** 5 minutes

¼ cup mayonnaise

½ cup sour cream

juice of ½ lemon

zest of ½ lemon

¼ teaspoon garlic powder

¼ teaspoon salt

¼ teaspoon pepper

½ cup blue cheese, crumbled

¼ cup buttermilk

1. To a small mixing bowl, add the mayo, sour cream, lemon juice, lemon zest, garlic powder, salt, and pepper. Mix together. Fold in the blue cheese, then add the buttermilk, a little at a time, stirring continuously, until the dressing reaches your desired consistency. Add more blue cheese to taste.

Thousand island Dressing

This sweet and savory dressing is great on Reuben sandwiches and patty melts.

MAKES: 2 cups | **PREP TIME:** 5 minutes

1 cup mayonnaise

3 tablespoons sweet pickle relish

½ cup sweet chili sauce

¼ teaspoon onion powder

½ teaspoon garlic powder

½ teaspoon paprika

squeeze of lemon juice

½ teaspoon salt

¼ teaspoon pepper

1. Mix all of the ingredients together in a medium bowl and taste. Adjust to your liking. Refrigerate until ready to serve.

Creamy Avocado Dressing

This creamy guacamole-style dressing is for avocado lovers. It's great on salads or as a dipping sauce for sandwiches.

MAKES: 3 to 4 cups | **PREP TIME:** 10 minutes

3 avocados

1 cup Greek yogurt

½ cup mayonnaise

1 bunch cilantro

3 stalks green onions

1 teaspoon garlic, minced

1 tablespoon white wine vinegar

¼ teaspoon cumin

1 teaspoon salt

¼ teaspoon pepper

juice of ½ lime

1 tablespoon extra-virgin olive oil

1. Add all the ingredients except for the olive oil to a food processor or blender, and pulse until well combined.

2. Pour in the olive oil and continue to pulse until the dressing is emulsified. Refrigerate until ready to serve.

Tartar Sauce

There is just something special about homemade tartar sauce. It's creamy, it's savory, it's sweet, and it's the perfect companion for beer-battered cod or fish fillet sandwiches.

MAKES: 2 cups | **PREP TIME:** 10 minutes

1 cup mayonnaise

6 bread-and-butter pickles, chopped

2 teaspoons bread-and-butter pickle juice

1 teaspoon dried dill or 1 tablespoon chopped fresh dill

½ teaspoon Worcestershire sauce

2 teaspoons Dijon mustard

¼ teaspoon salt

¼ teaspoon pepper

1. Add all the ingredients to a medium mixing bowl and mix the ingredients together until well combined. Refrigerate until ready to serve.

White Barbecue Sauce

White barbecue sauce, also known as Alabama white sauce, is sweet, smoky, and savory. You can use it as a basting sauce, a serving sauce, or even a marinade with any meat, but my favorite is chicken.

MAKES: 1 cup | **PREP TIME:** 5 minutes

½ cup mayonnaise

2 teaspoons honey mustard

¼ teaspoon Worcestershire sauce

1 teaspoon apple cider vinegar

2 tablespoons brown sugar

1 teaspoon prepared horseradish

¼ teaspoon salt

¼ teaspoon pepper

¼ teaspoon smoked paprika

¼ teaspoon garlic powder

¼ teaspoon cayenne pepper

squeeze of lemon juice

1. Place all the ingredients in a medium mixing bowl and stir together until well combined. Refrigerate until ready to serve.

Cajun Remoulade

Traditional remoulade sauce originated in France. Cajun remoulade, popular in Louisiana, adds a spicy Creole flair to this sauce. This remoulade is great served with seafood, such as crab cakes, or fried veggies, such as fried green tomatoes or fried pickles.

MAKES: 1 cup | **PREP TIME:** 5 minutes

½ cup mayonnaise

2 teaspoons Dijon mustard

1 tablespoon ketchup

2 teaspoons hot sauce

1 teaspoon blackened or Cajun seasoning

1 clove garlic, minced

1 tablespoon chopped fresh parsley

1. Place all the ingredients in a small mixing bowl and stir together until well combined. Refrigerate until ready to serve.

CHAPTER SIX

i CAN'T BELiEVE iT HAS MAYO!

Grilled Cheese

These warm, melty, and crispy grilled cheese sandwiches are
ready to be dipped into a bowl of tomato soup.

MAKES: 2 sandwiches | **COOK TIME:** 5 minutes

4 tablespoons butter, divided

¼ cup mayonnaise

4 slices of thick sliced bread,
such as Texas Toast

4 slices sharp cheddar cheese

1. In a pan or griddle large enough to fit the bread, heat 2 tablespoons of butter and begin to melt at medium heat.

2. Spread a thin layer of mayo (about one tablespoon) on one side of each piece of bread, and place the bread in the pan, mayo side down. Cook for 1 minute, or until, the bread is golden brown then flip.

3. Add one slice of cheese to the toasted side of each piece of bread and cook for an additional minute.

4. Flip the cheese side of a piece of bread onto the cheese side of another piece of bread to make a sandwich. Continue cooking, adding in more butter as needed, flipping occasionally until both sides of the sandwiches are browned and toasted. Serve immediately.

> Step up your grilled cheese game by adding meat, adding veggies, or using fancy cheese! For a lobster grilled cheese sandwich, add cooked lobster and use Gruyère cheese. For a BLT grilled cheese sandwich, add cooked bacon strips, lettuce, and tomato, and use sharp cheddar cheese.

Crab Cakes

Crab cakes made from fresh jumbo lump crab with panko breadcrumbs to hold it together, seafood seasoning, and a little lemon juice to wake it all up are simply delicious! These are great to eat right away or freeze to save for later.

MAKES: 8 crab cakes | **PREP TIME:** 10 minutes, plus 30 minutes to freeze | **COOK TIME:** 5 minutes

¼ cup mayonnaise

2 tablespoons Dijon mustard

1 teaspoon hot sauce

½ teaspoon Worcestershire sauce

1 egg, beaten

1½ teaspoons seafood seasoning

squeeze of lemon juice

1 pound jumbo lump crab meat

1 green onion stalk, green and whites chopped and hairy bottom discarded

2 cups seasoned panko breadcrumbs

2 cups canola or vegetable oil, for frying

1. Add the mayo, Dijon mustard, hot sauce, Worcestershire sauce, beaten egg, seafood seasoning, and lemon juice to a large mixing bowl. Stir until well combined.

2. Next, gently fold the crab, green onion stalk, and breadcrumbs into the wet ingredients, mixing just enough to combine all the ingredients. Note: Be careful not to overmix or break the crab.

3. Use a circular mold or your hands to form circular crab cakes, and place them on a freezer-safe dish. Put them in the freezer for 30 minutes, or refrigerate them overnight to allow the patties to get firm.

4. When ready to eat, pour canola or vegetable oil into a medium to large frying pan and heat over medium-high heat. Once the oil is hot, gently lay the crab cakes in the pan and fry for 2 minutes on each side or until the crab cakes turn golden brown.

5. Remove from the pan and place on paper towels to drain any excess oil. Serve immediately with Cajun Remoulade (page 105) or your favorite dipping sauce.

> **Pro Tip:** To make crab cakes ahead of time, place uncooked crab cakes in a freezer-safe bag, and store them in the freezer for as long as 2 months. When ready to cook, let thaw in the refrigerator, then cook according to the recipe instructions.

Bang Bang Shrimp

Crispy shrimp coated in a delicious sauce is a win-win kind of meal. It's sweet and savory, and the sriracha gives it that bang bang spicy kick! The sauce is great for completely coating popcorn shrimp but can double as a dipping sauce for larger butterfly shrimp.

MAKES: 2 to 3 servings | **PREP TIME:** 5 minutes | **COOK TIME:** 10 to 12 minutes

2 (12-ounce) packages or 1 (18-ounce) package frozen popcorn shrimp

3 tablespoons mayonnaise

½ cup sweet chili sauce

2 tablespoons agave nectar or honey

2 tablespoons sriracha or hot sauce

dash of red chili flakes (optional)

squeeze of lime juice

green onions, thinly sliced, for garnish

1. Preheat the oven to 450°F.

2. Line a baking sheet with parchment paper or foil, and spread the popcorn shrimp on top. Cook for 10 to 12 minutes or until the shrimp begins to crisp and turn brown. Remove from the oven and set aside.

3. To a large bowl, add the mayo, sweet chili sauce, agave nectar or honey, sriracha or hot sauce, red chili flakes, if using, and lime juice. Mix together. Add the popcorn shrimp and gently toss until each piece of shrimp is coated with sauce.

4. Top with the green onions and serve immediately!

Chicken Pot Pie

This pot pie is composed of flaky, buttery biscuits and a hearty mix of chicken and vegetables in a creamy sauce. I love making pot pies on refrigerator clean-out days. It's a great way to use crisper drawer vegetables and leftover chicken.

MAKES: 6 to 8 servings | **PREP TIME:** 10 minutes | **COOK TIME:** 30 to 40 minutes

1 tablespoon extra-virgin olive oil

2 chicken breasts, diced

1 teaspoon minced garlic

2 sprigs thyme

1 teaspoon smoked paprika

½ teaspoon salt

½ teaspoon pepper

1 white onion, finely diced

2 carrots, finely diced

2 stalks, celery finely diced

½ cup chicken broth

1 (10.5-ounce) can cream of mushroom soup

1 (10.5-ounce) can cream of chicken soup

2 tablespoons Garlic-Herb Mayo (page 19)

squeeze of lemon juice

1 (16-ounce) tin refrigerated biscuit dough

1. Preheat the oven to 350°F.

2. Heat a medium or large pan over medium-high heat, and add the extra-virgin olive oil. Once the pan is hot, toss in the chicken breasts and sear for about 5 minutes, until the chicken begins to brown.

3. Add the garlic, thyme, smoked paprika, salt, and pepper, then cook for an additional 2 minutes. Remove the chicken from the pan and set aside.

4. To the same pan, add the onion, carrots, and celery. Cook for 5 to 7 minutes, stirring occasionally, until the veggies begin to soften.

5. Add the chicken broth, cream of mushroom soup, cream of chicken soup, and mayo. Stir well.

6. Add the chicken back into the pot, along with a squeeze of lemon juice, and give the contents of the pot another stir.

7. Transfer the contents of the pot into an oven-safe baking dish, then top with the biscuit dough. Cook in the oven for 20 to 25 minutes or until the biscuits are browned and cooked through. Serve hot.

Barbecue Chip-Crusted Chicken Tenders

Chicken tenders crusted with crushed barbecue potato chips! This dish will blow your mind and have you wanting more. Serve with barbecue sauce or your favorite chicken tender dipping sauce.

MAKES: 8 to 10 tenders | **PREP TIME:** 10 minutes | **COOK TIME:** 25 minutes

2 to 3 (8- to 12-ounce) bags of your favorite barbecue potato chips (mine are Grippo's)

⅓ cup mayonnaise

¼ cup barbecue sauce

2 chicken breasts

½ teaspoon salt

½ teaspoon pepper

1. Preheat the oven to 400°F.

2. Place the barbecue potato chips in a food processor and pulse to a fine crumb. Transfer to a freezer bag. If you do not have a food processor, place the chips in a freezer bag, seal, and crush the chips with your hands or a can.

3. In a small bowl, mix the mayo and barbecue sauce, and set aside.

4. Next, cut the chicken breasts into 1- to 2-inch slices to create tenders. Season both sides liberally with salt and pepper.

5. Set a baking rack on a baking sheet. Place each tender in the bag with the chips, and shake to fully coat each piece. Now place the coated chicken tenders on the baking rack.

6. Place the baking rack and baking sheet in the oven and cook for 25 minutes, flipping the tenders halfway through the baking time. Continue baking until the chips are crispy and the tenders are cooked through.

7. Serve alongside your favorite dipping sauce, with celery and carrots.

> **Pro Tip:** Not a huge fan of barbecue chips? Then use your favorite chips instead. You will get the same crunchy result but with a flavor you love!

Roasted Chicken Quarters

Juicy, *flavorful*, and *downright delicious* are a few words that come to mind when describing this recipe. Let me introduce you to the moistest baked chicken you will ever have in your life! The herb butter helps keep the chicken juicy on the inside, and the herb mayo helps bring out the flavor and crispiness of the skin. This is a great weeknight dinner option and is best served alongside a grain, such as rice or rice pilaf, and a green vegetable.

MAKES: 3 or 4 chicken quarters | **PREP TIME:** 10 minutes | **COOK TIME:** 60 to 70 minutes

8 tablespoons (1 stick) salted butter, softened

2 teaspoons minced garlic

1 tablespoon chopped Thai or sweet basil

1 tablespoon chopped fresh parsley

1 tablespoon chopped fresh thyme

1 teaspoon white wine vinegar

juice of ½ lemon

1 teaspoon smoked paprika

1½ teaspoons salt

½ teaspoon pepper

3 or 4 chicken quarters

1 cup Garlic-Herb Mayo (page 19)

1. Preheat the oven to 400°F.

2. To a small mixing bowl, add the softened butter, garlic, Thai or sweet basil, parsley, thyme, vinegar, and lemon juice; mix together until well combined. Set aside.

3. To another small bowl, add the paprika, salt, and pepper. Mix together.

4. Lift the skin of the chicken quarters and spread the herb butter under it; do this for all the chicken pieces. Then sprinkle the paprika, salt, and pepper mixture on the outside of the chicken. Give the chicken a good rubdown to make sure the mixture sticks to the skin.

5. Place the chicken, skin side up, on a baking sheet lined with foil, nonstick paper, or parchment paper. Cover with foil and cook in the oven for 25 minutes.

6. Remove the chicken from the oven, and crank the heat up to 425°F. Place the chicken on a baking rack, and place the rack on the baking sheet. Spread the Garlic-Herb Mayo on the skin side of the chicken and on the bottom of the chicken (if you have enough). Place in the oven and continue baking for an additional 35 to 45 minutes, until the skin is crispy and the chicken is cooked through. Note: The chicken should reach an internal temperature of at least 160°F.

7. Remove from the oven and serve immediately.

Mayo-Pesto Seared Steak

Yes, mayonnaise can be used even on steak! This version is similar to steak topped with chimichurri. You still get the taste of steak, but also a lot of flavor from all the ingredients in the pesto. This is great served alongside mashed potatoes for the ultimate steak dinner. It's worth a try for a steak lover or anyone who loves a good piece of beef.

MAKES: 2 steaks | **PREP TIME:** 5 minutes | **COOK TIME:** 10 minutes

2 New York strip steaks, about 1 inch thick

½ teaspoon salt per side

¼ teaspoon pepper per side

¼ cup mayonnaise

3 tablespoons basil pesto

1 tablespoon minced garlic

squeeze of lemon juice

2 tablespoons extra-virgin olive oil

sprinkle of salt, to serve

1. Rinse each steak under lukewarm water, then use a paper towel to pat dry. Place the steaks on a dish and season both sides liberally with salt and pepper; set aside.

2. To a small bowl, add the mayo, basil pesto, garlic, and lemon juice. Mix together until well combined and set aside.

3. Heat a medium or large cast-iron pan over medium-high heat. Pour in enough olive oil to cover the bottom of the pan. When the pan begins to produce a faint amount of smoke, then it is ready for your steak. Coat the steak with a layer of the mayo-pesto mixture, then drop it into the pan. Cook for 3 minutes on each side.

4. Flip the steak onto its edge, and cook for an additional 1 minute (Note: Use a thermometer to check the internal temperature; see the list that follows this recipe.) Remove from the pan and let rest for a few minutes before cutting.

5. Slice the steak against the grain and finish with a sprinkle of salt. Serve immediately.

Pro Tip: Measure the internal temperature of the steak by inserting a thermometer into the thickest part of the steak and pushing it to the middle.

STEAK COOKING TEMPERATURES

Rare—125°F, very red inside, cool interior

Medium rare—135°F, red inside, warm interior

Medium—145°F, pink inside, warm interior

Medium well—150°F, slightly pink inside, warm interior

Well—160°F, no pink inside, warm interior

Pimiento Cheese Drop Biscuits

Red Lobster has some of my favorite drop biscuits. These pimiento cheese biscuits are remarkably similar to the Red Lobster biscuits and are great to make when you have some extra pimiento cheese or cheddar cheese.

MAKES: 8 biscuits | **PREP TIME:** 10 minutes | **COOK TIME:** 20 to 25 minutes

2 cups self-rising flour

3 tablespoons Pimiento Cheese (page 47)

3 tablespoons cold salted butter

1 cup buttermilk

½ cup melted butter, for topping

2 teaspoons chopped fresh parsley, for topping

1. Preheat the oven to 400°F.

2. To a medium mixing bowl, add the flour and pimiento cheese. Stir together. Use a cheese grater to grate 3 tablespoons of cold salted butter into the flour mixture. Then pour in the buttermilk, and stir until all the ingredients are combined and a dough is formed.

3. Sprinkle a little flour onto a flat surface and place the dough on it. Pat down the top of the dough with a little flour. Divide the dough into eight even sections, and roll each section into a ball. Coat a baking dish with butter and place the balls in it.

4. Place the baking dish in the oven, and bake for 20 to 25 minutes until the biscuits rise and are browned.

5. Melt butter and add in the parsley, then brush it over the biscuits after cooking. Serve immediately.

Chocolate-Mayo Cupcakes

There have been way too many times I have wanted to bake a cake or cupcakes, but did not have eggs or oil. Because mayonnaise contains both egg and oil, it is good to use for those ingredients should you ever be without either.

MAKES: 18 cupcakes | **PREP TIME:** 10 minutes | **COOK TIME:** 21 to 24 minutes

2 cups all-purpose flour

2 teaspoons baking powder

½ cup cocoa powder

1 cup brown sugar

¼ cup granulated sugar

1 cup mayonnaise

1 teaspoon pure vanilla

1 cup half-and-half

1 cup milk chocolate chips

16 ounces premade chocolate icing

1. Preheat the oven to 350°F.

2. Combine the flour, baking powder, and cocoa powder in a medium mixing bowl.

3. To a large bowl, add the brown sugar, granulated sugar, mayo, vanilla, and half-and-half, use a hand mixer and blend together until all the ingredients are well combined. Add the dry ingredients to the wet ingredients, and mix until all the ingredients come together.

4. Add the milk chocolate chips to a small microwave-safe bowl, and cook on high for 30 seconds. Stir the cholate chips and cook for another 30 seconds. Stir again. Once the chocolate has melted, add it to the batter.

5. Line the cupcake tins with the paper baking cups (if you don't have paper baking cups, spray the cupcake tin with nonstick cooking spray). Add the batter evenly to the paper baking cups, filling them up only about halfway.

6. Place the cupcakes in the oven, and bake for at least 20 minutes but no longer than 23 minutes. Remove the cupcakes from the oven, and place them on a cool surface. Let the cupcakes sit until they are cooled.

7. Once they are completely cooled, remove from the tin and top with the chocolate icing.

CHAPTER SEVEN

MAYO HACKS

Mayonnaise shows off its versatility in the kitchen—but its usefulness doesn't stop there. Here are four of my favorite ways to use mayo outside the kitchen.

HAIR CONDITIONER

Mayonnaise is a great conditioner for your hair, adding shine and strengthening the hair follicles. Mayo contains eggs, which are a great source of protein and also contain proline, an amino acid needed to produce collagen. Both protein and collagen will strengthen not only your hair but also your bones. Place a generous amount of mayonnaise on damp hair and let sit for 30 minutes to let the hair absorb the nutrients. Then rinse well under cool water, and follow up with your normal shampoo and conditioning routine.

CUTICLE SOFTENER

Take your at-home manicure to the next level by showing some love to your cuticles. If you are like me, you don't always have cuticle oil lying around whenever you need to get busy on those cuticles or hangnails. But mayonnaise is almost always readily available and doubles as a great cuticle softener. Just add about ½ cup of mayonnaise to a small bowl and soak your fingers in the mayo for 10 minutes. Rinse with warm water, then use your manicure tools to push back your cuticles.

HOUSEPLANT CARE

Houseplants are great for removing dust particles in the air, but the dust gets trapped on the surface of their leaves, which can begin to look dull. Use mayonnaise to add shine to the leaves. Water your potted plant, then wipe the leaves with a damp paper towel. Next, add mayonnaise to another paper towel, and gently wipe the leaves again. Voilà!

STAIN REMOVER

Mayonnaise can also be used as a stain remover. Crayon on the walls? Mayo can help with that! Water stain on wood? Mayo can help with that too!

To remove crayon from the walls: Run a cloth under warm water, then spread a small amount of mayo on it. Rub the crayon marks. Continue rubbing, adding more mayo to the cloth if necessary, until the marks are removed.

To remove water stains on wood: Add a bit of mayo to a cloth, then apply the mayo directly to the water-stained area. Let the mayo sit overnight, then wipe it away with a clean cloth. (Note: Try this on a small amount of the stained area to test that no further damage will be done. If it passes this test, apply mayonnaise to the entire damaged area.)

CONVERSIONS

VOLUME CONVERSIONS

US	US. Equivalent	Metric
1 tablespoon (3 teaspoons)	½ fluid ounce	15 milliliters
¼ cup	2 fluid ounces	60 milliliters
⅓ cup	3 fluid ounces	90 milliliters
½ cup	4 fluid ounces	120 milliliters
⅔ cup	5 fluid ounces	150 milliliters
¾ cup	6 fluid ounces	180 milliliters
1 cup	8 fluid ounces	240 milliliters
2 cups	16 fluid ounces	480 milliliters

WEIGHT CONVERSIONS

US	Metric
½ ounce	15 grams
1 ounce	30 grams
2 ounces	60 grams
¼ pound	115 grams
⅓ pound	150 grams
½ pound	225 grams
¾ pound	350 grams
1 pound	450 grams

TEMPERATURE CONVERSIONS

Fahrenheit (°F)	Celsius (°C)
70°F	20°C
100°F	40°C
120°F	50°C
130°F	55°C
140°F	60°C
150°F	65°C
160°F	70°C
170°F	75°C
180°F	80°C
190°F	90°C
200°F	95°C
220°F	105°C
240°F	115°C
260°F	125°C
280°F	140°C
300°F	150°C
325°F	165°C
350°F	175°C
375°F	190°C
400°F	200°C
425°F	220°C
450°F	230°C

RECIPE INDEX

ABOUT THE AUTHOR

Creativity comes in many forms, and for Erin Isaac, it touches on her greatest passion: cooking. Erin thrives in her roles as a recipe developer, food photographer, and founder of Slight Kitchen Werk by sharing her passion through her food and recipes. She has acquired her cooking skills from her grandmother, her parents, and more than a decade of experience. Erin is a multi-award winner for her innovative recipes at the Ohio State Fair. As a Cleveland, Ohio, native, these awards are some of her proudest accomplishments.

Erin's favorite cooking companions are her Infused Olive Oil (which is a product she developed and sells), music (preferably loud), and wine, preferably dry. When Erin is not in the kitchen, she loves to explore and travel. She enjoys trying new restaurants and taking cooking classes both locally and abroad, to learn about different cultures and cuisines, and to continuously perfect her craft. Erin is inspired by the many flavors of the world and uses these eclectic ingredients to re-create memorable recipes in her kitchen.

© Olivia Smith